Franklin D. Roosevelt

By Wil Mara

Consultant
Nanci R. Vargus, Ed.D.
Assistant Professor of Literacy
University of Indianapolis, Indianapolis, Indiana

Children's Press®
A Division of Scholastic Inc.
New York   Toronto   London   Auckland   Sydney
Mexico City   New Delhi   Hong Kong
Danbury, Connecticut

Designer: Herman Adler Design
Photo Researcher: Caroline Anderson
The photo on the cover shows Franklin D. Roosevelt.

Library of Congress Cataloging-in-Publication Data

Mara, Wil.
  Franklin D. Roosevelt / by Wil Mara.
    p. cm. – (Rookie biographies)
Summary: An introduction to the life of the thirty-second president, Franklin D. Roosevelt, whose three terms in office spanned the years of the Depression and the Second World War.
Includes bibliographical references and index.
  ISBN 0-516-21844-1 (lib. bdg.)   0-516-25823-0 (pbk.)
  1. Roosevelt, Franklin D. (Franklin Delano), 1882-1945–Juvenile literature.
2. Presidents–United States–Biography–Juvenile literature. [1. Roosevelt, Franklin D. (Franklin Delano), 1882-1945. 2. Presidents.] I. Title. II. Series: Rookie biography.
  E807.M28 2004
  973.917'092–dc22

                              2003013690

CHILDREN'S PRESS, and ROOKIE BIOGRAPHIES®, and associated logos are trademarks and or registered trademarks of Scholastic Library Publishing. SCHOLASTIC and associated logos are trademarks and or registered trademarks of Scholastic Inc.
5 6 7 8 9 10 R 13 12 11 10 09 08   62

Franklin D. Roosevelt was the thirty-second president of the United States.

Roosevelt was born on January 30, 1882, in Hyde Park, New York. His family was rich.

For many years, Roosevelt went to school at home. His family taught him to care about other people.

Roosevelt met his wife,
Eleanor, in college.

Eleanor worked with poor
people in New York. She cared
about other people, too.

Roosevelt had a famous cousin. His cousin was Theodore Roosevelt. Theodore was the twenty-sixth president of the United States.

Theodore Roosevelt

Franklin D. Roosevelt

Theodore helped Roosevelt to decide to run for office. Roosevelt thought he could help many people this way.

In 1910, Roosevelt ran for senator (SEN-uh-tor) in New York. He won.

A senator is someone who helps make laws.

14

In 1921, Roosevelt got sick. He got a disease called polio (POH-lee-oh).

After that, he had to use a wheelchair. That did not stop his work.

In 1928, people in New York made Roosevelt their governor (GUHV-uh-nor). A governor runs a state.

Roosevelt did a good job. He helped many people who did not have jobs.

Roosevelt became president of the United States four times.

The first time was in 1933. Many people could not find work at that time.

Roosevelt found ways to help these people.

Slowly, things began to get better. Then Roosevelt had another problem to solve.

In 1941, the United States joined a war. The country fought against Japan, Germany, and Italy.

The United States worked with other countries to win the war. Many people died. It was a sad time.

In 1945, Roosevelt became president for the fourth time.

By this time, Roosevelt was very sick from many colds. Yet he kept working to end the war.

Roosevelt went to his home in Georgia to rest. He died there on April 12, 1945.

The war ended soon after Roosevelt died.

Roosevelt was a great president.

29

Words You Know

run for office

polio

president of the United States

senator

Theodore Roosevelt

Index

About the Author

More than fifty published books, including biographies, bear Wil Mara's name. He has written both fiction and nonfiction, for both children and adults. He lives with his family in northern New Jersey.

Photo Credits